Girls For The Win!

Girls on the SOFTBALL TEAM

Beth Gottlieb

Enslow PUBLISHING

DISCOVER!

Please visit our website, www.enslow.com. For a free color catalog of all our high-quality books, call toll free 1-800-398-2504 or fax 1-877-980-4454.

Library of Congress Cataloging-in-Publication Data
Names: Gottlieb, Beth, author.
Title: Girls on the softball team / Beth Gottlieb.
Description: New York : Enslow Publishing, 2023. | Series: Girls for the win! | Includes index.
Identifiers: LCCN 2021046430 (print) | LCCN 2021046431 (ebook) | ISBN 9781978528208 (library binding) | ISBN 9781978528185 (paperback) | ISBN 9781978528192 (set) | ISBN 9781978528215 (ebook)
Subjects: LCSH: Softball–Juvenile literature. | Softball for women–Juvenile literature.
Classification: LCC GV881.15 .G67 2023 (print) | LCC GV881.15 (ebook) | DDC 796.357/8–dc23/eng/20211023
LC record available at https://lccn.loc.gov/2021046430
LC ebook record available at https://lccn.loc.gov/2021046431

Published in 2023 by
Enslow Publishing
29 E. 21st Street
New York, NY 10010

Designer: Katelyn E. Reynolds
Interior Design: Tanya Dellaccio
Editor: Kristen Nelson

Photo credits: Cover (girl) Rob Marmion/Shutterstock.com; cover (series artl) LHF Graphics/Shutterstock.com; p. 5 Monkey Business Images/Shutterstock.com; p. 7 (inset) ClassicStock/Alamy Images; p. 7 (main) Everett Collection/Shutterstock.com; pp. 9, 21 Sue Ogrocki/AP Images; p. 11 kali9/iStockphoto.com; p. 12 Pete Pahham/Shutterstock.com; p. 13 Oleksandr Panasovskyi/Shutterstock.com; p. 15 Pixel_Pig/iStockphoto.com; p. 17 Ken Mellott/Shutterstock.com; p. 19 Paul Sancya/AP Images; p. 20 Matt Slocum/AP Images.

Portions of this work were originally authored by Amy B. Rogers and published as *Girls Play Softball.* All new material this edition authored by Beth Gottlieb.

Printed in the United States of America

Some of the images in this book illustrate individuals who are models. The depictions do not imply actual situations or events.

CPSIA compliance information: Batch #CSENS23: For further information contact Enslow Publishing, New York, New York, at 1-800-398-2504.

CONTENTS

Boldface words appear in Words to Know.

PLAY BALL!

Softball is a **popular** sport for girls and women to play. In fact, girls can start playing when they are young children! It's a safe, fun team sport that teaches players to work hard together. Are you ready to join the team?

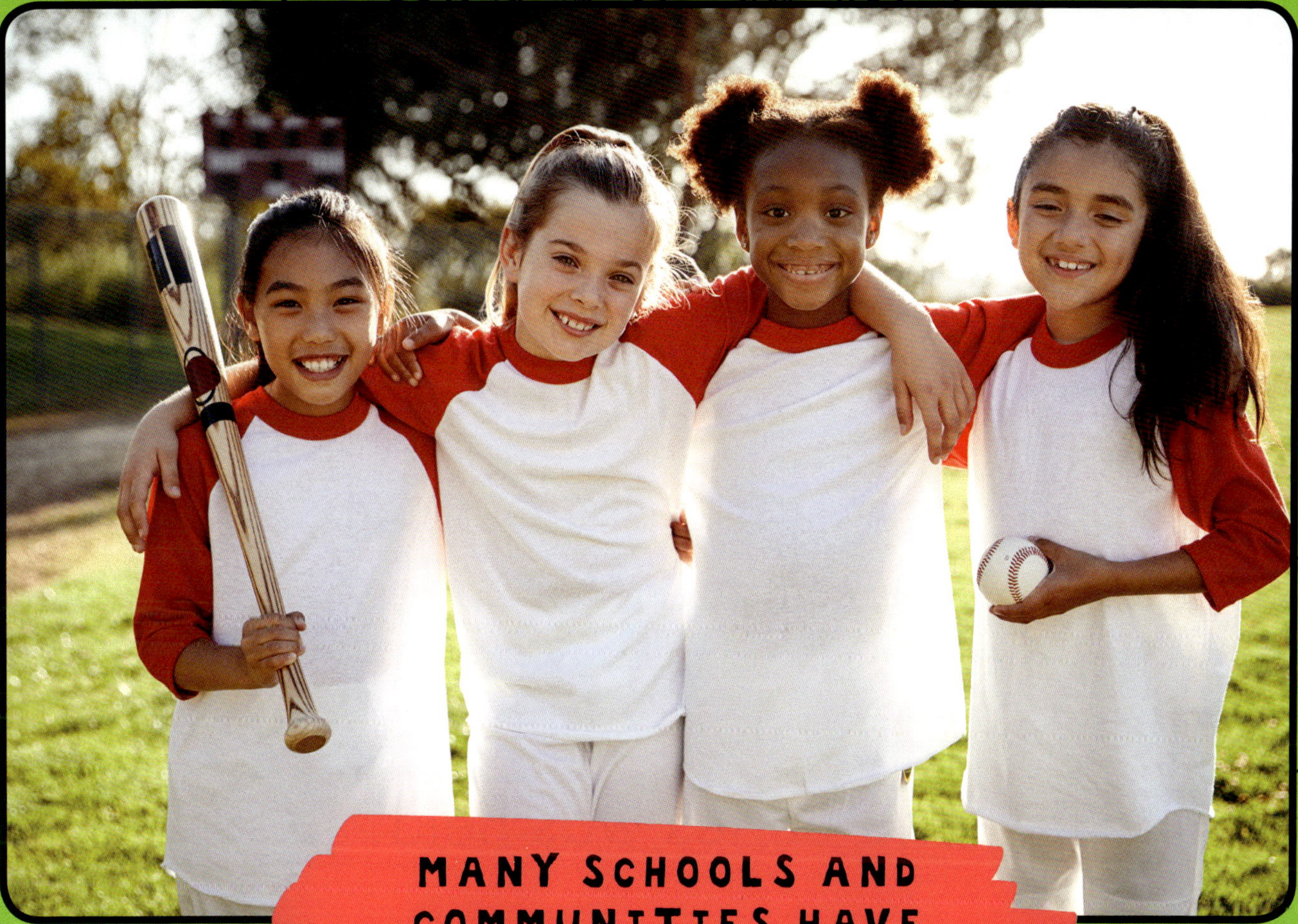

MANY SCHOOLS AND COMMUNITIES HAVE SOFTBALL **LEAGUES** FOR GIRLS AND WOMEN!

A LITTLE HISTORY

It's thought that the first softball game was played in 1887 in Chicago, Illinois. The sport grew starting around the 1930s. Women began playing in greater numbers by the 1950s. In 1969, the first Women's College World Series was held.

FOR A LONG TIME, PEOPLE BELIEVED SPORTS WERE TOO HARD FOR WOMEN TO PLAY. WE KNOW BETTER NOW!

WHAT'S THE DIFFERENCE?

Softball is a lot like baseball, but there are some important differences. In softball, the ball is bigger, the field is smaller, and the games have fewer innings. Also, baseball **pitchers** throw the ball overhand, while softball pitchers throw underhand.

THERE ARE TWO MAIN KINDS OF SOFTBALL: SLOW-PITCH AND FAST-PITCH. THE SPEED OF THE PITCHES IS THE BIGGEST DIFFERENCE BETWEEN THE TWO.

GET ON THE FIELD

In order to win a softball game, one team must score more runs than the other. Softball teams have nine or 10 players on the field at a time. How many depends on what kind of softball it is and the age of the players.

THE TENTH PLAYER ON SOFTBALL TEAMS OF YOUNGER PLAYERS IS AN EXTRA **FIELDER**.

Softball games have seven innings. In each inning, both teams have a chance to bat, or hit the ball, and play in the field. The team in the field is playing defense. They are trying to get batters from the other team out and stop them from scoring runs.

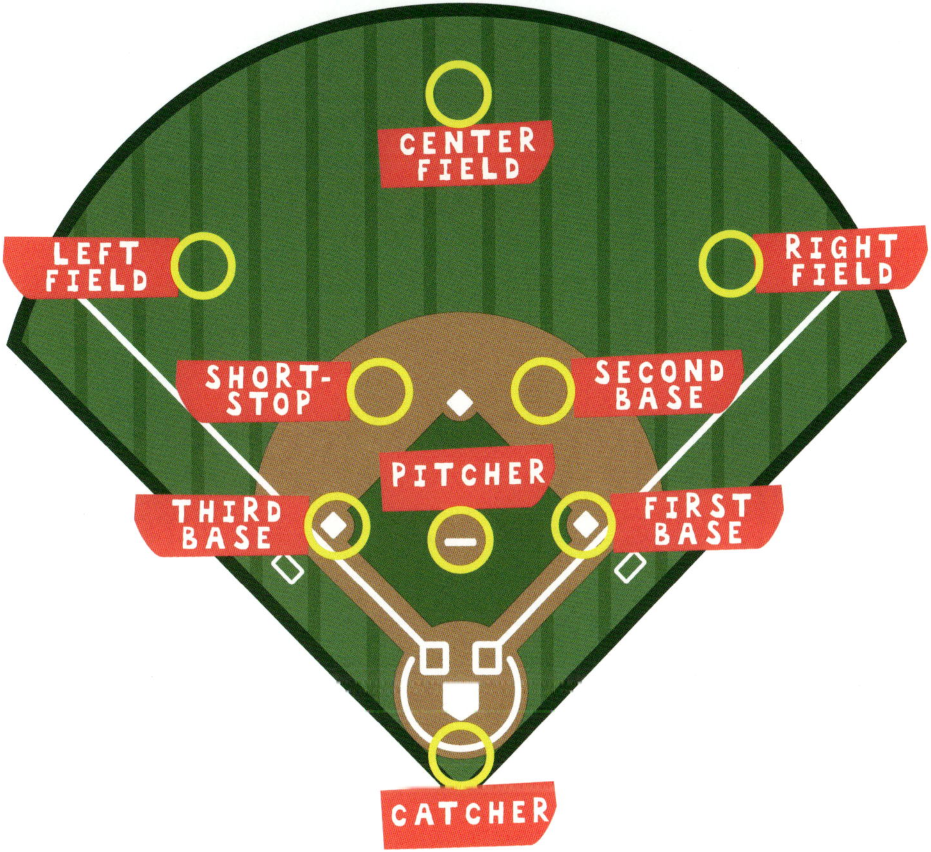

WHEN IN THE FIELD, THESE ARE THE POSITIONS PLAYERS ON A SOFTBALL TEAM PLAY.

RUNS AND OUTS

A batter tries to hit the ball with her bat after the pitcher throws it to her. If a player hits the ball, she has to run to first base. She can keep running to the next bases if she thinks she can make it.

WHEN THE BALL IS HIT, THE BATTER TRIES TO MOVE ALL THE WAY AROUND THE BASES TO SCORE A RUN.

If the batter doesn't hit the ball, that's a **strike**. Batters who get three strikes are out. A batter is also out if a hit is caught in the air. A batter who is tagged with the ball before she reaches a base is out too.

"TAGGED" BY THE BALL MEANS "TOUCHED" BY IT.

TOP PLAYERS

Softball is a major college sport for women to play. The Women's College World Series is the yearly college softball **championship** in the United States. National Pro Fastpitch was a **professional** softball league for women in the United States.

JENNIE FINCH WAS A GREAT COLLEGE PLAYER WHO WENT ON TO PLAY FOR TEAM USA SOFTBALL!

AT THE OLYMPICS

Women's softball became an **Olympic** sport in 1996. But, it was not in the 2012 or 2016 games. In 2021, women's softball returned to the Summer Olympic Games in Tokyo, Japan. Team USA won a silver **medal**!

JANIE REED

2021 USA WOMEN'S SOFTBALL

IT'S UNCLEAR IF SOFTBALL WILL REMAIN AN OLYMPIC SPORT. IT'S SO POPULAR WITH GIRLS AROUND THE WORLD, MANY PEOPLE THINK IT SHOULD!

Words to Know

championship A contest to find out who's the best player or team in a sport.

fielder A player who is in the field while the opposing team is batting

league A group of teams that play the same sport and compete against each other.

medal A flat, small piece of metal with art or words that's used as an honor or reward.

Olympic Having to do with the Olympics, the international athletic contests that occur once every four years.

pitcher The player who throws the ball to the batter in softball.

popular Liked by many people.

professional Having to do with a job someone does for a living.

strike A pitch that passes through a certain area over home plate without being hit and that counts against the batter.

FOR MORE INFORMATION

Books

Buckey, A. W. *Women in Softball*. Lake Elmo, MN: Focus Readers, 2020.

Downs, Kieran. *Softball*. Minneapolis, MN: Bellwether Media, Inc., 2021.

Websites

Little League Softball

www.littleleague.org/play-little-league/softball/

Do you want to find or start a softball team? Learn about Little League Softball on this website.

Softball Facts

www.softschools.com/facts/sports/softball_facts/793/

Read more fun facts about the game of softball.

Publisher's note to educators and parents: Our editors have carefully reviewed these websites to ensure that they are suitable for students. Many websites change frequently, however, and we cannot guarantee that a site's future contents will continue to meet our high standards of quality and educational value. Be advised that students should be closely supervised whenever they access the internet.

INDEX